EXTREME SUMMER
SPORTS ZONE

SKATEBOARDING STREET

Patrick G. Cain

Lerner Publications Company • Minneapolis

Lerner Publications Company
A division of Lerner Publishing Group, Inc.
241 First Avenue North
Minneapolis, MN 55401 U.S.A.

Website address: www.lernerbooks.com

Content Consultant: Jorge Angel, Skatepark of Tampa Event Coordinator

Library of Congress Cataloging-in-Publication Data

Cain, Patrick G.
    Skateboarding street / by Patrick G. Cain.
        p.   cm. — (Extreme summer sports zone)
    Includes index.
    ISBN 978–1–4677–0749–7 (lib. bdg. : alk. paper)
    1. Skateboarding—Juvenile literature. I. Title.
GV859.8.C34 2013
796.22—dc23   2012029415

Manufactured in the United States of America
1 – BP – 12/31/12

Photo credits: The images in this book are used with the permission of: Backgrounds: © Sean Justice/Getty Images, 5; © Paul Archuleta/Getty Images, 6; © Stephen Bonk/iStockphoto, 7; © AP Images, 8, 9; © Rex Features/AP Images, 10; © Robert Abbott Sengstacke/Getty Images, 11; © Kevin Winter/Getty Images, 12; © Christian Pondella/Getty Images, 13; © Mark J. Terrill/ AP Images, 14, 25; © Patricia Metcalf/Shutterstock Images, 15; © Bret Hartman/AP Images, 16; © Lad Strayer/AP Images, 17; © Denis Nata/Shutterstock Images, 18; © Shutterstock Images, 19, 29; © M. Dykstra/Shutterstock Images, 20-21; © Milosz Aniol/Shutterstock Images, 21; © Jared Wickerham/Getty Images, 22; © Arena Creative/Shutterstock Images, 23; © Bigstock, 24; © Lori Shepler/AP Images, 26; © Jeff Gross/Getty Images, 27; © Harry How/Getty Images, 28

Front Cover: © Harry How/Getty Images; © RTimages/Shutterstock.com (background).

Main body text set in Folio Std Light 11/17.
Typeface provided by Adobe Systems.

Some photos in this book depict athletes skateboarding without safety gear. The publisher strongly encourages all skateboarders to use standard safety gear at all times.

TABLE OF CONTENTS

CHAPTER ONE

WHAT IS SKATEBOARDING STREET?

In 1977 skateboarding was still a new sport. At that time, the sport's home was Southern California. Ten-year-old Rodney Mullen lived in Florida—on the other side of the country. Skating wasn't common there. But Rodney still wanted to learn how to skateboard. Rodney's dad thought the sport looked dangerous. Mr. Mullen was right. Skateboarding can be dangerous. But he also knew Rodney could skateboard safely if he was careful.

The father and son made a deal. Rodney could have a skateboard if he always wore his knee pads. He also had to quit if he got injured. Rodney Mullen would go on to create the style of skateboarding known as street. He invented more than 30 moves. Kids still do Mullen's moves when they practice on streets and sidewalks.

Safety gear is still an important part of skateboarding street.

SAFETY FIRST!

Street skateboarding can be a dangerous sport. Learning a new trick or practicing an old one can lead to a hard fall. Still, many skateboarding street competitions, including the X Games, don't require athletes to wear helmets while competing. Even though you might not always see the skaters on TV wearing helmets and pads, this safety gear is very important to avoid injury. For a pro, a bad fall can mean the end of a career. For an amateur skater, a rough fall can mean giving up a favorite hobby. So whether skating for a competition or for fun, street skaters should always wear the proper safety equipment.

5

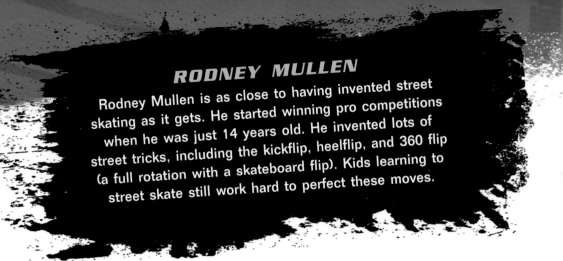

RODNEY MULLEN

Rodney Mullen is as close to having invented street skating as it gets. He started winning pro competitions when he was just 14 years old. He invented lots of street tricks, including the kickflip, heelflip, and 360 flip (a full rotation with a skateboard flip). Kids learning to street skate still work hard to perfect these moves.

Millions of kids and adults across the United States skateboard. When skaters step on skateboards for the first time, they are street skating. Street skaters use their boards to navigate up, down, and around street obstacles. With practice, these skaters learn to jump their boards on curbs and up and down stairs. They slide down railings. They hop up on benches. Professional skaters also skate on street courses. These pros use park benches, handrails, and stairs to do a series of tricks. Street skating is very different from vertical (vert) skating. Vert skaters use half-pipe ramps to do tricks.

Rodney Mullen is one of the pioneers of street skating.

Skate parks feature everyday objects, such as railings and stairs. Street skaters use them to create tricks.

Street skateboarding has influenced fashion, music, television, and video games. It has even changed the way city streets and parks are designed. Some major cities have parks designed especially for street skaters. These parks have small ramps, railings, jumps, and stairs right next to one another. Street skateboarding has big brands, star athletes, and huge competitions. It's a great time to be a kid with a skateboard!

CHAPTER TWO

STREET'S EARLY DAYS

Skateboarding wasn't always cool. In the early 1900s, a skateboard was nothing more than roller-skate wheels attached to a wooden board. In the 1950s, surfers picked up the sport. The first commercial skateboard was sold in 1959. These early boards had metal wheels. Eventually, clay wheels replaced the metal ones. But the wheels often broke or locked up in the middle of a trick.

Surfers helped make skateboarding popular.

Skateboarding got a lot more popular during the 1970s.

The first skateboarding competition was held in 1963. Still, skating was mostly for kids. No one thought of it as a professional sport. But everything changed in the 1970s.

The Z-Boys

In 1975 the company Bahne Skateboards held a major skate competition called the Del Mar Nationals. A little-known skate team from Southern California took the event by storm. The team was called the Zephyr Competition Team. It was made up of a group of surfers who had taken up skateboarding.

The Zephyr skaters were known as the Z-Boys. The Z-Boys had a rebellious attitude and a creative spirit. They trained in empty pools. They did moves inspired by surfing. Their moves were wild. They skated like there were no rules. They skated unlike anyone else. Big sponsors soon picked up the Z-Boys. Their unusual style was the future of skateboarding.

Skateboards in the 1970s switched to polyurethane wheels. These wheels were sturdier than clay wheels. The new wheels glided more smoothly over city streets. This improvement helped riders push the limits of their tricks. In the mid-1970s, young Florida skater Alan Gelfand invented an exciting new move. He used a curved wall at a skate park to jump his board without grabbing on to it. In 1977 former-Z-Boy Stacy Peralta witnessed the trick. Peralta was amazed. The move became known as the ollie, which was Alan's nickname.

The ollie is one of the most important tricks in street skating. Some experienced street skaters can even ollie over objects.

Mike Vallely does an ollie trick at Spike TV's 2008 Video Game Awards.

Peralta quickly offered 15-year-old Alan a place on his team. The trick opened the door to countless future moves. In 1982 Rodney Mullen did the first ollie from flat ground. Skaters began doing ollies over curbs and other obstacles. In the late 1980s, skaters like Mike Vallely and Mark Gonzales continued pushing street skating into the future. They invented new tricks that drew new fans to the sport.

MIKE VALLELY

Mike Vallely, known as Mike V., was one of the top riders in the 1980s. His daring moves often landed him on the cover of major skateboarding magazines such as *Thrasher*. He was known for bringing vert-style tricks to street skating. Mike V. no longer skates in competitions. But he is still active in the skateboarding world. In 2011 he agreed to help his former sponsor Airwalk redesign its classic skateboarding shoes.

By the mid-1990s, skateboarding street was becoming a mainstream sport. Cable sports network ESPN was there to help. With the Extreme Games, ESPN brought street skateboarding into fans' living rooms. The event was later renamed the X Games. Skateboarding's popularity has continued growing. Street skaters keep creating daring tricks. They compete at major events like the X Games. Thanks to the Internet, skaters around the world can film themselves skating and post videos online. Fans can watch street skating whenever they want.

Manny Santiago competes at the 2012 X Games skateboarding street finals.

CHAPTER THREE

STREET CULTURE, EQUIPMENT, AND MOVES

Street skateboarding allows skaters to express themselves with their own moves and tricks. But the creativity isn't limited to competitions. The sport's edginess has given rise to its own culture. Skateboarding is known for its gear, brands, clothing, music, and art. Skateboarding athletes star in video games, movies, television shows, commercials, and more.

Street skaters like Lacey Baker use their individual style to create awesome tricks.

Street skaters usually wear sturdy and comfortable shoes and casual clothing they can move easily in.

The Brands and the Style

Skateboarders wear jeans, T-shirts, hoodies, and sneakers. The clothing is comfortable and easy to move around in. In the 1980s, Bill Mann designed a shoe specifically for skateboarding. He built the shoe to handle the tough tricks a skater would put it through. He called the shoe the Airwalk, after the famous trick of vert hero Tony Hawk. The shoe was an instant success. Airwalk became a company that sold skateboarding clothing and accessories. Eventually, Airwalk sponsored its own skate teams.

VIDEO GAMES

Vert skateboard legend Tony Hawk helped spread the sport to millions of skating rookies. But he did so off the street. In 1999 he made the first of his 16 very popular video games, *Tony Hawk's Pro Skater*. The game was a huge hit. Legendary snowboarder and vert skateboarder Shaun White launched his own street skating game in 2010. *Shaun White Skateboarding* was made for the Wii console. The game was also very popular with fans.

Other brands soon became popular with skaters, including Vans, Emerica, Element, Birdhouse, etnies, and Zoo York. These brands modeled their products on what skateboarders were already wearing. They became important sponsors of individual skateboarders. Sponsors support skaters financially so they can focus on learning new tricks. Sponsors also help put on major competitions that bring together the best skaters.

Etnies is one of the companies that sponsors street skater Ryan Sheckler.

These skateboard designs inspired by Native American art were displayed at the Smithsonian's Ramp It Up exhibit.

Music and Art

Music has always been an important part of skateboarding. For a long time, skateboarding was associated with punk rock and other fast-paced styles of music. This music's fast tempo and spirit fit the skaters' style. Many skaters also listen to hip-hop music when they skate. Their videos use hip-hop as the background music.

The visual arts have also had an impact on skateboarding. In 2009 the Smithsonian Institution opened Ramp It Up: Skateboard Culture in Native America. This exhibit traveled around the country for years. It showcased the positive effects of skateboarding in Native American and Hawaiian cultures. In 2011 a Los Angeles, California, dance company put on *Transit Space*. The dance company drew inspiration from the moves and style common in the world of skateboarders.

Safety

Staying safe is the most important part of skateboarding street. Street skateboarders can only get better if they stay healthy. Learning a new trick often means taking spills. Even pros have hard falls during practice and competitions. Street falls can be very dangerous. Injuries can also ruin skaters' careers. If a pro gets seriously injured, that pro may not be able to skate. The skater could lose sponsors. As a result, most pros wear safety gear whenever they skate. Pro street skaters say you need this gear to stay in one piece:

No matter how much a skater practices, falls happen in street skating.

The right safety gear means a skater can often get back on his or her board after a spill.

Helmet: A skater should wear a helmet no matter what his or her skill level is. Most pro skateboarders use bowl helmets. These helmets are made of a hard plastic material. Bowl helmets often have different colors and graphics on them.

Knee pads: Many street skaters land on their knees when they fall. Wearing knee pads gives a skater a better chance of getting up to try that trick again.

Elbow pads and wrist guards: When taking a spill, a skater often extends his or her arms to break the fall. Without elbow pads and wrist guards, a skater can get serious arm and hand injuries.

BREAKDOWN OF A SKATEBOARD

WHEELS

Wheels need to be extra sturdy. If a wheel breaks or falls off during a trick, a skater could be seriously injured. Most wheels are made of tough polyurethane. Wheels come in different hardnesses. Harder wheels slide more easily over smooth surfaces. Softer wheels are better for bumpy surfaces. Street skaters usually prefer harder wheels.

TRUCKS

The trucks connect the deck to the wheels. The trucks allow riders to lean on the deck's sides so the deck tilts. The tilt helps the skateboard make smooth turns. Trucks come in different sizes. A wider truck makes it easier to turn and grind (slide along an obstacle). A smaller truck makes it easier to do flip tricks.

DECK

A skateboard's deck is the main body of the board. A skateboard deck needs to be very tough to hold up to street tricks. Skateboard makers often use six or seven layers of wood or manmade materials when making the deck. Decks come in many different shapes and sizes. Street skaters usually prefer a narrow deck for the tricks they do.

GRIP TAPE

Grip tape covers the top of the deck. Its sandpaper-like surface gives skaters traction on their boards. Skaters can lean more deeply and land tricks more easily if their feet do not slip off the deck.

PAUL RODRIGUEZ

Mexican American skater Paul Rodriguez (sometimes known as P-Rod) was the first skateboarder to be sponsored by Nike. He is also one of the best skaters in street. He won the 2012 X Games street competition. This victory was nothing new for P-Rod. In 10 years, from 2003 to 2012, P-Rod won six X Games medals in street. Four of those medals were golds.

The Moves

The street tricks a pro can do on a skateboard are almost unlimited. An amateur skater usually starts by practicing basic tricks. After skaters learn a few basic moves, they can try tougher tricks. Many skaters put two or more tricks together to create a combination of tricks, known as a combo. Here are a few moves all the pros started with.

Grind: In a grind, a skateboarder first jumps the board off the ground. Then the skater lands the board on an obstacle, such as a handrail. The board and the skater slide along the obstacle until the obstacle ends or the skater jumps the board off the obstacle. Skaters do many different types of grinds.

Paul Rodriguez does a grind at a competition in 2012.

Kickflip: A kickflip begins on flat ground. But instead of keeping the feet planted, a skater kicks the feet off the board. The skater then uses the toes to flip the board in the direction in which the toes are pointed. After the flip, the skater lands both feet on the board.

Heelflip: A heelflip is a lot like a kickflip. But instead of using their toes to flip their boards, skaters use their heels. The board flips in the opposite direction of a kickflip.

Ollie: The ollie is one of the most important street tricks at any level of riding. To ollie, a skateboarder makes the board jump while keeping his or her feet planted on it. Skaters can do this off flat ground or off a ramp. With practice, a skater can ollie over obstacles such as curbs. The ollie is the foundation for almost every street trick.

CHAPTER FOUR

GOING PRO

Street skateboarders skate because they love the sport. Most skaters will never have the opportunity to go pro. Still, with enough hard work, a skater may get invited to a competition. But to get invited, a skater must get noticed.

Getting noticed isn't easy. A skater must win smaller competitions and pick up sponsors. That can be tricky. Some skaters do tricks at skate parks. They hope a pro or a possible sponsor will see them. The Internet can be a big help in bringing unknown skaters to new audiences.

If a skater does well enough at smaller competitions, he or she may have a shot at being a pro street skater.

Elissa Steamer competes at the 2006 X Games skateboarding street finals.

Many skaters tape themselves doing tricks and put the videos online. If their tricks are really good, people will notice. They may get invited to competitions. At the competitions, they may pick up sponsors. Getting sponsored brings a skater one step closer to going pro.

WOMEN'S STREET COMPETITIONS

Women's street events are just like the men's events. But the path to making it as a pro can be more difficult for a woman. Sponsors are much more active in the men's events. And the men's events are often more popular with fans. As a result, a female skater often can't make a living as a pro. In fact, in 2011 ESPN canceled the women's skateboarding vert competition. Not enough women were participating in the event. However, many great female skaters have caught the attention of fans. Elissa Steamer is one of the most successful women in street history. She has won four X Games gold medals in the street competition. Skaters Amy Caron, Alexis Sablone, Marisa Dal Santo, and Leticia Bufoni also win competitions. They wow fans and judges with their awesome tricks.

Team Riding

Most professional skateboarders skate on teams. But these are not like the teams in sports such as football. Skateboarding teammates have the same sponsor and often practice together. But in skateboarding street, everyone competes individually. Skaters on the same team may even skate against one another in a competition.

Nyjah Huston skates for the Element team, but he competes individually.

Competitions

Many skateboarding street events take place throughout the year. Mountain Dew's Dew Tour occurs every year. Red Bull also hosts several competitions. The Tampa Am is one of the biggest amateur contests in street skating. Almost every pro has skated in the Tampa Am or its pro event, Tampa Pro.

Pro skater Leticia Bufoni competes at the 2009 X Games.

For most fans, the biggest street event of the year is the Summer X Games hosted by ESPN. Like the Olympic Games, winners earn gold, silver, or bronze medals. X Games winners also win prize money. Pro skaters often work for months trying to perfect a specific run (series of tricks). For that reason, many new tricks first appear at the X Games.

The X Games features both a men's and a women's event in skateboarding street. Women's skateboard street is one of the few Summer X Games events in which females can compete. Alexis Sablone won the gold medal in 2012 with a run that included a kickflip over a gap. It was her second gold medal. Veteran skater Paul Rodriguez won the gold medal in the men's event. It was his fourth gold medal, breaking the record for most street gold medals won.

Scoring

At a skateboarding street competition, skaters get a set amount of time to skateboard through a course. The course features obstacles like handrails, stairs, and ramps. The obstacles are designed to copy objects a skater may see when skating in the real world.

ALEXIS SABLONE

X Games gold medalist Alexis Sablone is showing the world that skateboarding street isn't just for men. She entered her first skate contest when she was 12 year old. She has been almost unstoppable ever since. She won gold medals at the 2010 and 2012 X Games. And she earned silver medals in 2009 and 2011. In 2008 she graduated from Barnard College with a degree in architecture and plans to continue school to earn a master's degree.

The 2012 X Games street course was based on a schoolyard. The course included a flagpole, stairs, a lunch table, and a handrail. Each skater had one minute to perform a run on the course.

The athletes use the course obstacles to do tricks. Judges rank each run on a 1 to 100 scale. Scores are based on the amount of tricks, the difficulty of the tricks, and how smoothly the skater performs them. Each skater gets four runs. A skater's highest score counts as his or her final score. Sablone's winning score in 2012 was 85.66. Rodriguez's winning score was 86.00.

Where to Watch

ESPN and ABC networks both broadcast the X Games. But fans don't have to wait all year for amazing street tricks. Pros and amateurs post videos of themselves skating to video-sharing websites. Some of these videos help teach young skaters how to learn new tricks. A parent or other adult can help young fans track down these videos online. But remember—only try new tricks within your skill level!

It's important to start small when learning new street tricks. It takes a lot of practice to pull off the kinds of tricks pros do at the X Games!

GLOSSARY

AMATEUR

someone who participates in an activity for fun without expectation of payment

COMBO

a group of tricks done together

MAINSTREAM

something that is commonly accepted

PROFESSIONAL

someone who participates in an activity as a job for payment

ROOKIE

someone who is new to a sport or activity

RUN

a set of tricks

SPONSOR

a company that financially supports professional athletes in a sport so they can focus on that sport

TRACTION

gripping power to keep a skater from slipping

VETERAN

an experienced skater

FOR MORE INFORMATION

Further Reading

Braun, Eric. *Tony Hawk*. Minneapolis: Lerner Publications Company, 2004.

Cain, Patrick G. *Skateboarding Vert*. Minneapolis: Lerner Publications Company, 2013.

Doeden, Matt. *Shaun White*. Minneapolis: Lerner Publications Company, 2011.

Horsley, Andy. *Skateboarding*. New York: Rosen, 2012.

Thomas, Isabel. *Board Sports*. Minneapolis: Lerner Publications Company, 2012.

Websites

ESPN X Games
http://espn.go.com/action/xgames
The official X Games website features information about the X Games. Check out skateboarding street athlete bios, videos, and scores, and find out when and where the next X Games will be held.

How to Ollie on Your Skateboard
http://www.kidzworld.com/article/4445-how-to-ollie-on-your-skateboard
This website gives step-by-step instructions on how to ollie a skateboard. Remember to put on a helmet and pads before trying a new trick.

Learning How to Skateboard for Beginners for Kids
http://www.livestrong.com/article/433056-learning-how-to-skateboard -for-beginners-for-kids/
Check out this website for safety and technique tips to help rookie skaters the first time they get on their skateboards.

INDEX

About the Author

Patrick Cain is a nuclear engineer turned writer. He is an award-winning journalist whose work often appears in a number of magazines such as *ESPN the Magazine*, and *Fast Company*. He currently lives in Los Angeles, California, but will forever be tied to upstate New York.